WHAT IS
COVID-19?

By Sara Latta

The Child's World®
childsworld.com

Published by The Child's World®
1980 Lookout Drive
Mankato, MN 56003-1705
800-599-READ
www.childsworld.com

Photos ©: alinabuphoto/
Shutterstock.com: 19; Alonafoto/
Shutterstock.com: 9; Andrii
Vodolazhskyi/Shutterstock.com:
cover, 2; angellodeco/Shutterstock.
com: 5; Diego Cervo/Shutterstock.
com: 16; Jarva Jar/Shutterstock.
com: 13; JOKE_PHATRAPONG/
Shutterstock.com: 6; Photographee.
eu/Shutterstock.com: 10; YES
Market Media/Shutterstock.com: 15;
Shutterstock.com: 22

ISBN 9781503852761
(Reinforced Library Binding)

ISBN 9781503853232
(Portable Document Format)

ISBN 9781503853294
(Online Multi-user eBook)

LCCN: 2020939118

Printed in the United
States of America

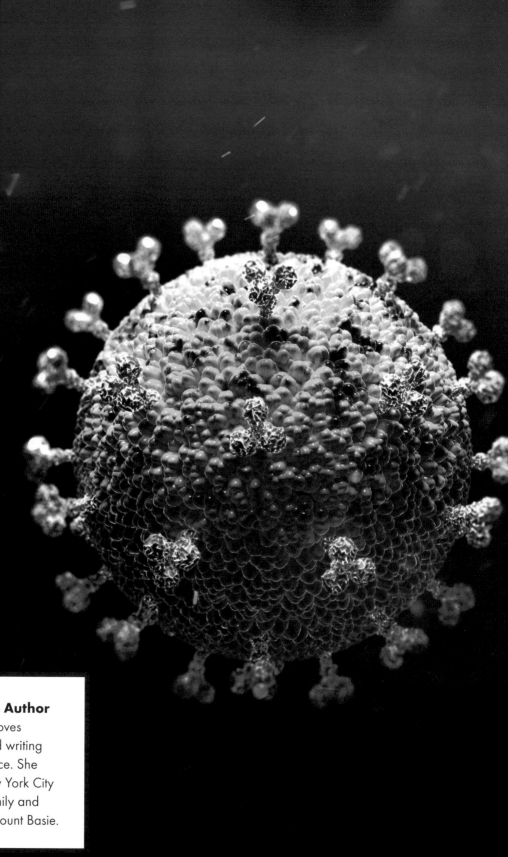

About the Author

Sara Latta loves reading and writing about science. She lives in New York City with her family and their dog, Count Basie.

CONTENTS

CHAPTER ONE
What Is COVID-19?   4

CHAPTER TWO
How Does the Virus Make People Sick?   11

CHAPTER THREE
How Can We Recognize and Treat COVID-19?   14

CHAPTER FOUR
How Can I Be Brave?   18

Think about It   21
Good News!   22
Glossary   23
To Learn More   24
Index   24

What Is COVID-19?

COVID-19 is the short name for "**CO**rona **VI**rus **D**isease 20**19**." It started in the year 2019. The disease is caused by a tiny germ, or **virus**. Scientists call it SARS-CoV-2. Most people just call it the "new coronavirus."

Viruses are too small to see without a powerful microscope. Some viruses can make us very sick. Others, like the ones that cause the common cold, just give us a mild illness.

The virus that causes COVID-19 is part of a large group of related viruses. They are all round, with crown-like spikes on their surfaces. The word *corona* means "crown" in Latin.

Scientists are learning more about COVID-19 every day. They share information with each other in hopes they can stop the disease soon.

Don't waste water while scrubbing! Turn on the water, get soapy, and then turn off the water during your 20 seconds of washing. Don't forget your wrists and the backs of your hands! Rinse your hands well when you're done.

One way the new coronavirus enters people's bodies is if it gets on their hands and then they touch their mouths, noses, or eyes. Try not to touch your face with your hands. It is important to wash your hands often, especially after you use the restroom and before you eat. But you knew that anyway, right?

COVID-19 FACT

Soap and water kill the virus. Wash your hands for 20 seconds. This is about as long as it takes for you to sing the "Happy Birthday" song twice!

Someone with the virus who coughs or sneezes without covering their mouth or nose could infect people standing nearby. Even speaking to another person might spread the virus. This is why people wear masks. Their masks protect you. Your mask protects others.

One of the best ways to prevent the spread of the virus is to avoid being around groups of people. This might mean you can't go to school or play with your friends. Sometimes protecting each other means staying apart for a while.

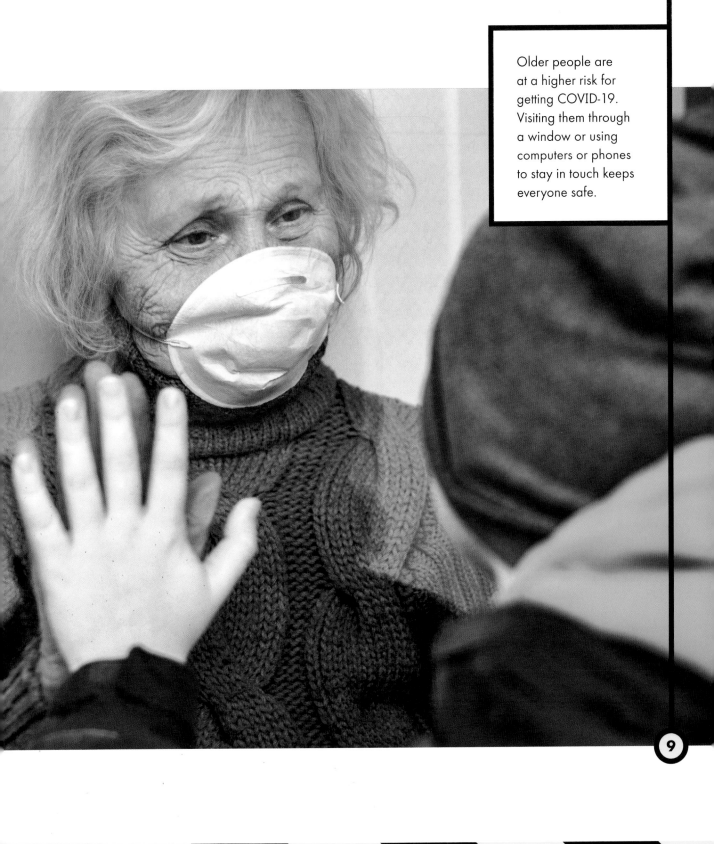

Older people are at a higher risk for getting COVID-19. Visiting them through a window or using computers or phones to stay in touch keeps everyone safe.

The early stages of the coronavirus often feel much like a common cold.

CHAPTER TWO

How Does the Virus Make People Sick?

The coronavirus invades cells in the nose and throat first. It uses the spikes on its surface to get inside the cells. Think of using a key to unlock a door. Once inside, the virus forces the cells to make new copies of the virus. These copies break the host cells open and go on to infect more cells.

At first, people infected with the virus may not feel sick at all. Or they might develop a cough, a fever, or head and body aches. Some people lose their senses of smell and taste.

The virus may make its way down the windpipe and to the lungs. It invades the cells that help transfer oxygen to the blood. The body has an army to fight germs like the coronavirus. This army is called the **immune system**. Blood cells in the immune system target and kill cells infected with the virus. They leave behind a stew of fluid and dead cells. This makes it hard to breathe. Some people develop a bad case of **pneumonia**. It may become deadly.

COVID-19 FACT

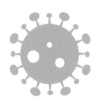

Scientists believe the virus came from wild animals. Somehow, the virus found its way from animals to humans. Now the virus has spread all around the world.

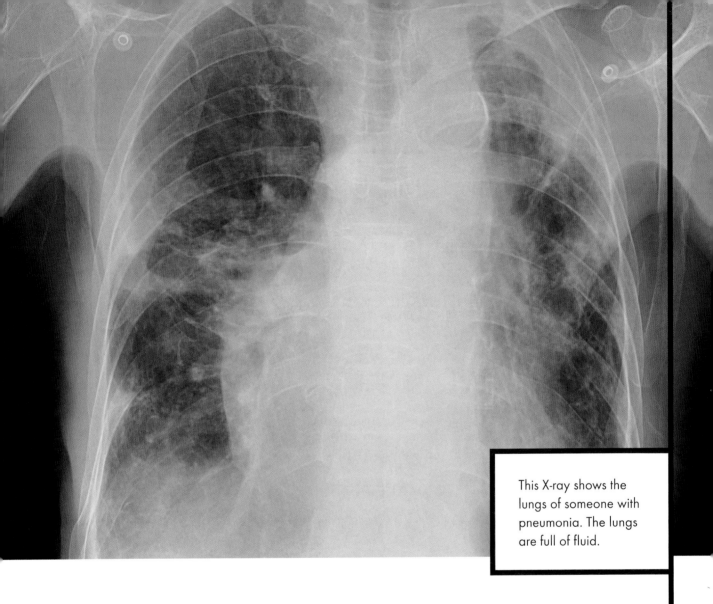

This X-ray shows the lungs of someone with pneumonia. The lungs are full of fluid.

The coronavirus sometimes travels to other organs. It can attack the heart, blood vessels, kidneys, and even the brain.

CHAPTER THREE

How Can We Recognize and Treat COVID-19?

If you have a fever, cough, or your head and body hurt, you may have COVID-19. There is a special test to see if you have COVID-19. Your parents can call your doctor to see if you need the test. If you do, a nurse will stick a cotton swab far up your nose to get a sample. They can test that sample for the virus.

Most people, especially children, have mild illnesses. Even if you are sick, you can probably stay at home. Your parents can help you prevent the spread of the virus at home.

The swab is like a long version of the ones you might have at home. The nurse needs to swab the back of your nose. Some people say it tickles!

Staying away from others when you're sick can be hard. But staying apart helps keep others healthy while you get better.

People who have COVID-19 should get plenty of rest. They need to drink lots of water or juice. They can take medicine to help lessen fever and pains. People who need to go to the hospital may get more oxygen through a tube placed in the nose. This helps them breathe.

A person has recovered from COVID-19 when they have been without a fever for at least 72 hours and they no longer have any other symptoms.

COVID-19 FACT

People with COVID-19 should try to stay away from others in their own home. Staying in a separate room helps keep other family members healthy. Even staying away from pets is a good idea until scientists know more about the disease.

How Can I Be Brave?

You might feel scared about getting sick. You may worry that people you love will get the disease or even die. It's okay to feel that way. A lot of grownups feel scared and worried, too.

Talk to a parent or caregiver about your feelings. They can help you understand what is going on. They can help you stay safe and keep others safe.

You can use some special tricks to help stay calm. Imagine you are holding your favorite flower. You can even hold a real flower if you have one! Hold it in front of you and breathe in through your nose for four seconds. It smells so good! Hold your breath for four seconds. Then breathe out through your mouth. Do this a few more times.

Drawing colorful pictures to hang in your window is a great way to spread happiness.

Pretend you are a feather. Flutter and float through the air. Then freeze! You are a feather statue. Unfreeze and float through the air again. Do this a few times. Make sure you end as a floating feather.

This hard time will not last forever. Scientists around the world are working hard to find new medicines that will help people sick with COVID-19 get better. They are trying to make a coronavirus **vaccine** that will prepare your immune system to fight the virus, like the shots you get to prevent other diseases.

Until then, find your own ways to stay brave. Dance. Jump rope. Read your favorite story. Do things that make you happy.

THINK ABOUT IT

There are lots of things you can do at home while keeping yourself and others safe.

1. Are you missing playing with your friends or hugging your grandparents? Make a card and ask a grownup to mail it to them.

2. Ask a grownup to help you make some cookies. You can share them with a friend or neighbor. You can put them outside their door. Ring the doorbell or knock. Then move far away from the door. Let them know you made them a treat!

3. Decorate paper masks with crayons or markers. Make them as silly or colorful as you like! Wear them whenever you go out.

People who have recovered from COVID-19 have **antibodies** in their blood. Antibodies are proteins made by cells in the immune system. They help fight the virus.

Some people who have had COVID-19 are giving blood to help others with the disease. The antibodies in the liquid part of the blood can be given to people who are sick. Doctors hope that their antibodies can help sick people fight the infection until their own immune systems can take over.

GLOSSARY

antibody (AN-tih-bah-dee) An antibody is a protein made by your cells in your immune system. Antibodies fight invading germs.

immune system (ih-MYOON SIS-tum) Your immune system is a collection of proteins, cells, tissues, and organs that work together to protect your body from germs and infections.

pneumonia (nuh-MOHN-yuh) Pneumonia is a disease that causes a person's lungs to fill with fluid. A person with pneumonia often has a fever, cough, and difficulty breathing.

vaccine (vak-SEEN) A vaccine is a weakened or dead form of a disease that is swallowed or injected into a person. This causes their body to fight the germs, and gives them the antibodies to fight that disease's germs if the body comes in contact with them again.

virus (VY-russ) A virus is a very tiny germ that causes diseases. A virus can only be seen with a special kind of microscope.

TO LEARN MORE

IN THE LIBRARY

Laughlin, Kara L. *What Is A Pandemic?*
Mankato, MN: The Child's World, 2021.

Laurence, Dorothea. *Paula and the Pandemic.*
Cheverly, MD: Dorothea Laurence, 2020.

Wallace, Adam M. *The Day My Kids Stayed Home: Explaining COVID-19 and the Corona Virus to Your Kids.* Adam M. Wallace, 2020.

ON THE WEB

Visit our website for links about COVID-19:

childsworld.com/links

Note to Caregivers, Teachers, and Librarians: We routinely verify our Web links to make sure they are safe and active sites. So encourage your readers to check them out!

INDEX

hand washing, 7
immune system, 12
infecting, 8, 11, 12
new coronavirus, 4, 7, 11, 12, 13, 20

pneumonia, 12
recovering, 17
staying at home, 14
test, 14
treatment, 14, 17

vaccine, 20
wearing masks, 8
worries, 18

24